Verses on Wings

Verses on Wings

A collection of poems in various humors

Khushhal Singh

PARTRIDGE
A Penguin Random House Company

To order additional copies of this book, contact
Partridge India
000 800 10062 62
www.partridgepublishing.com/india
orders.india@partridgepublishing.com

Contents

SECTION III: Poems to the Tenth Master

SECTION IV: Thoughts on Mortality

SECTION V: Something about Myself

SECTION VI: From History

SECTION VII: Sonnets

SECTION VIII: Limericks

SECTION IX: Haikus

About the Book

Here is a collection of poems that inspires and lifts the spirit to a world of laughter, bows to the Lord, has a vision of the great Preceptor, achieves balance and sanity and kicks away any depressing feeling out of life. And there're plenty of sonnets, limericks and haikus to delight the reader.

Dedicated to

Late Inderjeet Kaur
Whose Memory Ever Inspires Me

Acknowledgements

I am inspired by the Spirit of Love, and highly grateful to my dearest son Pushpendra Singh Matharu, my loving daughter-in-law Dipinder Kaur, and my charming grand-children Jasmine Kaur and Aman Preet Singh for their love, dedication and assistance all through the completion of the work.

Introduction

As the senior most of the new generation, I was rather over-pampered by my fond parents. They did not notice, perhaps did not even bother to notice the development, but neighbors did, and recommended skipping to curb the growing plumpness. I did attempt the rather girlish exercise, but a few skips and its thin rope would entangle to make me falter and fall. When I grew up to have some slight signs of black growth above the upper lip, and the sight of a girlie in a longish frock would push my pen to scribble a lyric, rhyming would prove a hurdle. So, though I loved to adorn my lines with rhymes, I treated rhyming a bore, as earlier I had treated the skipping rope. Hence I found it best to avoid this poetical ornamentation also. Blank verse, thus, became my favourite medium. The modern trend, I should like to believe, is also like mine.

I think the reader of today's mundane world, who needs a good bit of humor won't be disappointed in the book. He will have plenty of the stuff in these pages. Humor has its shades, and as a minor poet, I have various humors, at times looking up to the lofty Lord, sometimes pensive at life's passing show, and sometimes glowing with glory. On the whole, even from out of dark threatening clouds, hope and sunlight ever peep in. I am guided to sanity by the voice of the Greatest Optimist. That the reader too will get this healthy infection of mine is my poetic hope.

Khushhal Singh,
Brampton, ON, Canada.
khushhals@gmail.com

SECTION I

Poems in Light Vein

1. Those Good Old Days

Those were early days of nineteen sixty,
Just a few months after we were married,
When I was posted as a lecturer
In a new college in Butterton Town.
We had, first of all, to fix a small house,
But, for a two-room with a kitchen-bath,
The rent they demanded was ten bucks.
They said 'twas cheap, but we couldn't afford it.
The cost of kitchen items, and many more things
We needed, tho' not high, but poor me!
I did have not a very flattering salary,
Which just enough was to meet half basic needs.
At parents' place, I never had bothered ever
To see Dear Dad do the balancing act
With the budget, yet happy were our days and
Nights, being tension-free, for money was no worry,
And dear Dad would ever recoup all our needs.
I still remember a senior's comment:
"Beauty lies in eye of the beholder",
But promptly I said, "No, respected Sir,
Beauty lies in her *holder's ardent arms*".
And admired that old gentleman my age.
Those indeed were the good old days of youth!

2. My Future Plans

Let it not be thought that I a nut am,
Though some ambitious plans for my next birth
In my dreams I draw, and lest might I forget
Next morn, dreaming I video-tape these plans!
How I wish you could just see some of these,
So might you easily grasp their breadth and depth!
In the winged stork's bag, I plan to land
On earth, with a golden table-spoon in mouth
As the eldest obedient sonny of my fond
Affluent parents, and the brightest lad grow.
An athlete too—fastest, strong and shining.
After Oxford, would I at Berlin study
German, and at Paris my French.
A role-model for many many generations
To come, plan I lakhs of crores to make
Deserving poor of the world to educate.
They'll get slices with thick cow-butter!
As the Lord's man, will I sing and recite
Hymns, and by example preach the way to Him.
Though a townsman, shall I choose a village
Belle beautiful—simple, dimpled and smart
As my 'madam', who then will manage me!
Many Nobel-prizes would bestowed on me
Be for literature and civil services
To mankind. I will love too to hold laugh-
Shows to improve the mental health of man.
In a video, you'll find me elected
PM unopposed, without fighting for it.
This I cannot accept, and will only decline
Due to my many engagements the world over-
So many I will ever my wife's assistance need.
So for success of all our bright plans
Teams of helpers I sure shall need select-
Highly-qualified and top honest men.
(You know 'men' means chiefly 'women'.)

For this, you better download forms

From: www.A2Z.com.
Confident am I that no wise person
Dare call such a top meticulous person as
"Yours faithfully" a nut, unless he be one.
So pray I to God to grant you more brains,
And *heavenly Montek* approve my plans!
Note: Montek Singh is the famous Dy. Chairman, Planning Commission
of India.

3. On Computer I Compose

Happened it thus one morning,
Misplaced my fine hand-writing
I knew not where, nor could one find.
Advised my wife to use my mind
This time to see if it had gone
From the right hand to the left one,
Or from hand to one of my feet.
As usual, police failed to find it.
So, 'twas after many a thoughtless night,
Thought I did need computer byte,
As youth do to hide their bad hand.
I do type now thus to make amend.
Now do I the latest laptop use,
"Lap-dog" call it some to confuse.
Now have I many classics created.
"They're great", many critics have stated.
Read if you know*, but don't ever seek
An autographed copy; I am meek
Enough to confess my hand is worse,
Aren't these new gadgets quite a curse?
Note: *know' means know reading.

4. Forced to Drink

Once to a stag party, they invited me
And friends going there dragged me along.
Surprised was I to find no ladies there;
Wondered I if ladies relished not stags.
Ladies, they said, had gone elsewhere to attend,
In the same connection, their *hen* party.
How could a bachelor know such distinctions?
They were having a riotous time, with wine—
Fountains flowing and X jokes loudly told.
They spared me not, but dragged me away from
The rummy table to force rum on poor me.
Asked soda or water, poured I lots
Of water, till hardly any rum remained
In my tumbler. Yet I was down and out!
Water, water alone was there in the drink
I had that night, but don't they say excess
Even of the best can even a fish flatten!

5. Let Me Count the Days

Let me count the days I have with them spent.
Long back it was that gingivitis made me
Search out a dentist to cement back gums,
Who advised regular use of a medicated
Paste. This rubbed I, an obedient patient,
For full fifteen years on my diseased gums,
Till dropped one morn one upper incisor
Down to fubbing finger. That was the start
Of incisors, premolars, molars, and some other
Inhabitants of the cavity to loosen;
Some would just drop out. The next D.D.S.
Did at one sitting extract ten volunteers!
Efficiently fitted he the same moment
Instant dentures, filling vacancies well!
Came many more dentists, some one tooth or two
Teeth extracting. Thus was my old true set
By a set of brand new false teeth replaced.
In dentist's den, falsehood does defeat Truth!
Yet love I dentists. Know ye the reason?
For one, tho' now they give no laughing gas,
(Hardly I need any, for plenty I've my own.)
Yet they saved pain; the other reason was they
Prescribed, after extraction, religiously
Lavish supply of ice-cream, bricks of which
A mansion loved I melting in my mouth!
Amongst the thirty-two, sits wisest Wisdom.
A wonder 'tis, tho' mine was taken out,
Yet retain I still my marvelled WISDOM!

6. "Whom the Gods Love, Dies Young"

—Menander (That Philosopher of Old Old Days.)

That old man was completely transformed, when
Met I the fellow on my next visit
To his village, when thirty years later,
A function of the high school I attended.
Someone had come from his place to invite
Me to dinner that evening. Indded I
Was immensely surprised, for never had thought
i would ever meet him again, for the fellow was
On my earlier trip almost seventy-plus.
He was a person of healthy habits
No doubt—vegetarian who never took a sip.
He never did smoke, and was a widower with
No blemish of any affairs. Respected
Was he by one and all, and I too held
Him in high esteem. So did I agree
For dinner at his place, and reached before
Time to have a long chat with the old chap.
But I had the shock of my life to find
Things on the table before him I never
Had ever expected. There was Scotch and ice
With tumblers for three, and on his sofa close
To him reclined a smoking girl of twenty,
And also offering him a lighted cigarette.
Clumsy was her flimsy garb, and the room
With smoke was full. Uneasy felt I and asked
Ram Singh if we could hurry up the dinner.
When the girl went out, I showed my surprise
At the change in his life-style. The chap then
Explained: "I used to be quite optimistic,
Very religious, and God-fearing, and only thought
That God's favourite son was I, but then
Somewhere read Ithat "Whom gods love, dies young."
Aghast was I! Why all this austerity

Without being in the list of the best?
So now enjoy I my life as I please!"
I relished not a bit that night's dinner
In that dreary room of Mister Ram Singh,
With Scotch, smoke, and object of his young passion.

7. Jill and Gill

(A modernised nursery rhyme)

I've heard a nursery rhyme
Of small Jack and little Jill,
Who lived near a small hill.
They had done no crime,
But Dad asked them to hop
Up with speed to the top
To fetch a pail of water
(Isn't it a laughing matter?)
So they ran up the hill,
But some water did spill
On the way down the hill.
Way back it was poor Jack
Who on head got a crack,
For he tumbled and rolled
Down the hill, and, behold!
The boy wore no head-dress,
And so was in a mess!
Hence next time, Jill pick'd Gill,
(Never took Jack up the hill)
Gill was nice, paid all bills.
When he grew, the Sikh youth
Never went to shaving booth.
So when she grew, chose Gill
As her man, even up the hill.

8. My Heart Leaps Up When I'm Told

Mu heart leaps up when I'm told
The ground is by snow covered—
So 'twas when I was in Kulu;
So 'twas when I was married;
So in Canada as widower
See I snow melting into water,
As doth one's life melt into death.

A child is father of the Man
Or could be mother of the Woman;
And I wish my days to be
Bound as waves in a brook,
Or as pages in a book!

9. If Music be the Food of Love

(A Scottish Tale)

If music be the food of love, ration not
Its quantity, nor play out some rough tunes!
My heart overflows with feverish sentiments
For a voluptuous one of seventy four.
For centuries had I espied glimpses
Of that face, but her clansmen denied me
A single chat, rather threatened me with
Darts, daggers and arrows, and the brave me
For only her honour, had a noble retreat
Made. With the turn of fate, her third man's
Buried, and with my dearest Dad's demise
And will, I inherit all properties;
Hence her heart now is full of love for me.
So, ye bagpipers!
Play on all glad tunes,
And let us till morn finish this Scotch 'n' dance
All this while, till wedded are we next year,
After her brief bereavement period's over.
Age has made us both very patient indeed.
Till then, of course, the live-in relation.

10. Modern Polonius's Advice to Laertes

Listen,—my blessings follow thee!
And though respect you not my word very much,
Set in heart this chatter.—Let no girl steal
Thy peace or purse, thy credit or debit cards.
Be thou famous, yet try to be pompous
Never with any friend or unfriend, good or bad.
Grapple thou with no man, for forget not
A body muscular that thou should have had, rhou
Have not. Spend not much on eating out;
It injurious surely is, and friends
Could, like leaches, force thee to the bottle.
Give none thy ear; he might thy little brains steal.
Strut not in showy habit, for on Holi
Will be smeared and spoilt by hooligans,
Nor let fire-works on Divali pollute earth
Of ours. Better a borrower be, but never
Lend my hard-earned money to a friend, or
He shall then sure turn a foe unto thee.
This above all: to thine own self be true,
And it might follow that fright in danger
Must lead thou to the hastiest of flights!

11. Rama, Your Ganga isn't 'Mailee' (Dirty)

The melting glaciers into gushing waters, and
Then into cool river convert, for the sinners
Their bodies and souls to return home as
Purified, paying pundits their rightful dues,
Ganga its maternal respect, and to the
Society dinners to celebrate the event.
Thus do we 'nirvana'-wards move, snd by its
Catalytic power the holy Gangs holier
Runs on to the bay to dump our filth there.
None can check repeat 'dips' to clean us again.
We do gain some weight. Sure, some extra ego.

SECTION II

Poems to the Lord

1. A Buffoon's Babble

'Tis the truth! It is the only truth!
'Tis untrue that you alone are immortal,
For in reality we humans immortal
Are too. Hear, O God! Very loudly do I
Declare that I am more than your equal!
Think not that you've created humans,
For the fact is you our creation
Are, and that too in our image-
As Brahma, Vishnu and Mahesh
In India, and similar avatars else—where.
We have created and also baptized you!
You may to any temple anywhere go and
See for yourself how nicely have we
Chiseled you out of rocks, silver or gold
Into nice idols, flouting all your commandments.
Then do we instal, bathe, and adorn you, and
Make an exhibit in the temple to
Earn lots and lots of money, food and jewels.
Never think that we humans alone have an end;
Mind not if I tell you, my dear friend, that
You also die the moment that any of us
Forgets you, as it does so oft happen!
Do you know how many of us even disbelieve
In your existence, for you cannot be seen,
So say they that there's nothing like a God!
When we die, remember our sons 'n' daughters
Look up, and search us among the stars up above,
Beyond which have we been told you reside.
Our progeny build our memorials, and samadhis,
While no such thing reminds about your existence.
When you are angry, you send floods, earthquakes,
Thunder and pestilences, and what—not
And Kill innocent people; remember that
We too in wrath wage wars, murder, plunder,
And terrorize totally peaceful innocents.
Thus we too claim to be not any better!

But Thou as Bhagwan, Jehovah, Allah,
God, Waheguru, and by many other names
We worship in mosques, temples, churches!
Do you sometimes have, as we have so many times,
A headache, toothache, pain in your stomach?
Do you have high fever and call a doc?
Do you too, as we do, fall for damsels?
If such frailties trouble you not,
O my magnanimous Lord! ignore
These babbles of an old damn fool,
And pray, Lord, send him not to hell.

2. A Soulful Prayer

O Lord! Thou alone pervades all over,
Near or far, outside and within,
And deep in my heart and mind dwells.
Thou dost all our earthly needs meet.
Mercifully accept and grant me some space
Outside Thy door to sit and ever
On Thy Name in equipoise meditate.
May I all creatures of Thine love
And help as Thou dost me every way.
By Thy grace, the best of food 'n' drink
And tranquil mind I've. May I also
Man's faith enjoy, never forgetting
Thee, whether in pain or pleasure,
In rags or in rich silks blessed.
Forgive me, Lord, all sins of mine
Done, or thought of, and henceforth keep
Thy slave on a straight virtuous path.
Hearken, O Lord, this my prayer,
And shower peace all over the globe,
And banish man's hatred of man.

Thou art the only Supreme Prime Being,
Who even attends an unuttered cry.
Do allow, Lord, this prodigal's prayer.

3. Was He an Orphan?

One summer night a pleasant dream
Of a happy boy in tattered rags
Dawned, and knocked he on the door.
Thinking the boy was hungry, brought I
For him some food and cold water.
Suddenly there was a flash of light;
I found him in a regal costume!
Smiled he, "I have no teeth, and can't
Ever eat a thing". He said he had
No father, nor a mother, nor
An uncle, aunt, sister or brother.
No grandson, not had even a son,
But Himself's Father of all beings!
Of His own Will is He created;
Not of a woman is He born.
He can in any form or color
Anywhere appear, fearing none, and
Loving all of all castes, creeds, climes
Or land, church, temple or mosque.
He has no house, keeps no family;
A celibate, yet has created all.
No Yogi He, but He's Maha Yogi.
He's Shiva, no resident of Kailash,
But pervades in air, land 'n' water,
Controlling events over universes.

When I woke, lingered still that image;
Transformed was I, with peace within,
And a fresh, pious glow all around me!

4. As Man Adores His Creations

Once my friend Ram asked me why was it
That a hand, that from rock a deity sculpts,
Joins the other to worship his own creation.
Further asked he why, on similar ground,
Does God also bow not before each of us,
And all other creatures in His universes.
But he then felt we sculpted only a few,
While numberless are the things that He makes,
Breathes in, sustains, and does in the end,
Wrap up into Himself. I knew not then, nor
Know I even today if I could understand
Or any mortal can ever delve into the Truth.
So I felt 'twas best to silent remain.
Pretty as ants, yet do we go multiplying
Gods and goddesses, tho' the truth is that
We humans can never a little fly create!

5. Remembrance

O Power Supreme! O Thou Creater of all!
To Thee, address I this prayer, O Lord!
O Father! Forgive this Thy erring child
All unforgiveable lapses of his, and
Do accept him back in Thy blissful flock,
Cleansing his filthy sinful mind of all
Vanity of what he thought he created,
Or claimed as his, or thought he had a right to,
And had forgotten flesh wasn't the only thing.
Thus was he by the devil's forces possessed.
O Lord! Great is Thy Name, as Thyself art;
May Thy Name alone this heart's guide ever be!

6. A Joyful Day

While the day's yet many furlongs away,
Sounds yet the harsh alarm of the clock,
Reminding the old man how few
His days and nights on earth could be
Before begins his journey back Home.
A life of strife it might have been
Against disease, dismay and defeat,
Yet forgets he not the hours filled
With faith, fond love, truth and success.
Man's life a mix bag of pleasure
And pangs is, which with equanimity
Must man bear, ever thanking the Lord.

7. The Voice Within

Disclosed have saints a space within, where dwells
A voice ready to guide a man if cares he
To listen, when wavering. There's a curse, though
That swells his head so completely that treats
He the world, Harnakush-like, as his own
Heaven, where his dictates none must dispute,
Where he, God-like, creates in everyone a hell.
With this mental egoistic eclipse, he
Forgets that power, gold, armies, relations are
Nothing but transient, mere mortal material.
He forgets from sown weeds no roses bloom.
O my heart, do remember the voice within-
That Divine Light that'll ever the right path show.

8. The Best of All

Better than an infidel is a swine,
Which cleans up the town, while
The God-forgetter is soon forgotten.
Better is Thy servant than gravel,
That hurts the way-farer, while God's
Servant ought to be the dust of the earth.
Better would it be if he were like water,
For, as water, he will clean up the limbs
While, as dust, he flies and merely soils them.

'Tis no use if Lord's serf is like water,
That easily is cold or hot, for 'tis best
The serf is just like the Lord Himself.
Note: The thoughts are of Saint Kabir.

9. The Ignorant She-Gardener

How very ignorant are you, she-gardener
To think you serve the idol with leaves you pluck
For puja! Know ye not that leaves breathe, and
The stone-idol the world worships lifeless is?
Would it not have swallowed the sculptor, while
Sculpting, he had put his foot on "god's" breast?
Note: From a hymn of Saint Kabir against idol-worship.

10. In Gratitude

O Lord, because of you I breathe,
Have delicious food to eat, ceiling
Above my head, a family I call mine,
And every comfort of life—a car,
A job, and a social position.
Because of Thee am I so happy,
And my heart is so full of Thee.
All do ever respect Thy servant,
Who free is of disease; even when
Ill, Thy power never lets him down and out.
Thou dost keep my faults a secret.
Grant me that I never forget Thee!

11. Back to the Ocean

O this cruel heat evaporated has
Me against my will from my Father
Ocean for no fault of mine, so high
Up as tiny vapor in this cloud
I orphan-like feel agitated.

Oh, what's this? I'm now transformed
Into a raindrop, and with my friends
Descend into the valley below,
Cheering long-awaiting thirsty crowds,
Run on in brook, rivulet, and river,
Cultivating hungry fields, and bathing
Pilgrims, and with their blessings hurry
On to where revered Ocean awaits me.

12. Will Wounds Heal?

(Written child-like on hearing of the death of an anarchist)

A hope has this morn in my heart been born
That soon might the world's deep wounds be healed,
World'd death-dealers might eliminated be,
Dawning days of peace and love for gloomy
Sunsets of hatred and innocent bloodbaths.
For long have they to the peaceful men been
Destroyers of their lives, peace, livelihood
And hoped achievements—a threat to Allah's flock.

May soon the demons from earthly stage exit,
And brotherhood among humans all over prevail.
Hearken, O Lord, this my fervent prayer!

SECTION III

Poems to the Tenth Master

1. The Dust

How I long
the dust to be
under the foot
of the Master,
so might I
even to an eye
gone visionless
enlightment
Divine become.

The breath 'n' breeze
carrying the touch
of the Master
could reveal
to any person
all the truth.

2. His Message to the Lord

That great valiant hero
who lost had almost
all brave disciples,
also Ajit and Jhujhar,
and crossing over
their dead bodies
now here had come
and lies down alone,
not on any flowery
silken bed, but sleeps
on this thorny ground
with a rocky pillow,
yet in this stage
this yearning disciple
grateful is for all this
to his Lord, without
whom any greater
comfort is agony,
like living with
poisonous snakes.
Without the Lord, 'tis
like being under
a slaughterer's dagger.
With his Beloved Lord
feels he the pleasure
of a soft mattrss, but
without his Lord,
in a royal palace,
feels he as if he's
being burnt alive!

3. The Gift

What a gift that
wooden comb was
with few fallen hair
the Guru gave
Pir Budhu Shah
After Bhangani battle
that cost the Pir
two of his sons and
both his brothers!
But that gift did
his wife Nasiran
console, dispelling
the untruth of
everything of all
of the worlds.

4. He Shed No Tears

Has any mortal
ever lost a son
shedding no tears?
But my lofty Guru
himself proudly allowed
sons Ajit and Jhujhar
to fight and fighting
die sure death
in unequal battle
at Chamkaur, singing
only glory of the Lord.
Who would not term
such a heroic figure
a God, but forbade he
all from calling him
anything but the serf
of the 'Param Purkh'*
Lord, or face only
annihilation!
'Param Purkh' means Supreme Prime Being.

SECTION IV

Thoughts on Mortality

1. We Were Eleven

Every early evening, after walk in the Neighbors' Park,
We, the tired four, sit and discuss not politics,
But blood pressure, body-aches, and ever-rising prices,
Under-table fees for a new ration-card,
And relief love and devotion give ancient bones.
Unaware of kids, who unaware are they too will
Be as old as we're, and that once we were also as
Young too, sit we regaining our breath
somewhat, while they
Play around us, hardly taking note of anything else.
We, who were a group of eleven just ten years back,
Have lost to heart, kidney, and cancer five dear mates
And also many in families of ours, and two have gone
Back to Bengal, hence four of the group are left.
Our last chapter the Writer writes, and alone He knows
How many pages more of our books He wishes to pen.

2. Valentine

Just as I've for many years done,
This year also have I bought,
And sent a valentine card
To a close ancient friend.
I shouldn't call him 'friend'.
How very rude is the fellow
Who does never ever respond!
Neighbors often he visits,
And takes some person along
To some undisclosed place.
Sometimes has he brushed
Against me, but has left
Just muttering a 'Sorry',
Uttering not another word.
He came thief-like, eight years
Ago to our place and stole
My darling life-mate away.
So after that day have I
An appeal to the Almighty
Made, for know I so well
The fellow obeys Him alone.
On each date, do I await
That Court's final judgment.

3. Call of My Star

I know I must fly
High up in the Sky
Seen not by any eye.

I would, like a lark,
Disappear in the dark
With, on land, no mark.

Isn't it time for me
From all bonds to be
Like her, totally free?

Calls my darling star
To twinkle with her;
So must I fly afar.

4. Void

Fairest of sll fsiries at Fate's ordain,
Came to this earth, to be born grand-child
Of a saintly old man, who devoted himself
To her well-being, showering his blessings.
He chose for his grand-child a bright young man,
Wedded to books, till her charms cast a spell
On him. Her sweet and soft nature made her
Darling of her parents and in-laws alike.
She bore him a son like her own nature.
The fairy and her hubby romanced some time
Though they belonged to two such different worlds.
She ruled over whatever she did ever survey,
Making friends along. Soon, alas, came an urgent
Call from the land of the fairies, making
For my dearest Jeet's unwilling retreat.
Mourn I the void her going in my life's caused.
Her garlanded portrait my wet orbs watch
And ever remember our sweet good old days.

5. Ready for the Wolf?

Wolf-like, it stalks victims all over the world
All beings that tread, swim, or fly in the sky,
Dreading sudden painful panther-like kill.
It does pounce like a wily wild hyena,
Or like an unmissing enemy bullet.
We know not the minute of day or night,
Or the direction of the pouncing paw.
We know not, but the hour was fixed at birth
Or even before it, for merging with Him
That the Lord had communicated to us;
Ignorant, we know not His warrant's language,
And death, a mere servant, has options none.
Death's couriers pull sinners away by their hair.
For His saints, though, come comfortable palanquins.

6. Mother

Tears, the pious precious water on earth,
Have not come, when fell I down and cried
In pain, or her milk sought, or severely
Fell ill, and her comforting lap gave me
Relief more than any toy, or any other treat.
She made of me a man, and deepened
She my faith in all things holy and sublime.
How do I long that tranquil face to watch,
Her soft feet to touch, and in her hug
To be compressed! No more, O God!
Where to find Thee now that Thou hast
So suddenly recalled her from earth?
Amidst this crowd, how very lonely do I feel!

7. On M.F. Hussain's Demise

It has come so to pass no more his brush
Any nude shall paint, nor shall he be forced out.
God's in His Heaven, and peace reigns on earth!

The Supreme Painter, who ever in colors
New His worlds repaints, had drums of many dyes
Bestowed on the charmed man, blessing him with skill
To go on a spree and to spray canvases,
Cans, cups, saucers, everything with figurines
No eye would tire gazing on joyful figures
Of beauty against beastly carnal sculptures
Outside famed temples of tourist interest.
The Lord never nude gods and goddesses has
Sent, but men do undrape them in their brains.
Brigades that can't lift brush rush to punish.

8. OTHELLO

O thou moor, what hast thou done?
T hy Desdemona lies dead!
H ie thee and with her be one
E re she might tell more lies.
L ovest thou as she doth still.
L o! The moor now flees away
O ff to clasp again his lady.

9. The Red Rose

O thou rose of red hue!
Like verses is thy morn
When thy petals unfold
And enchanting fragrance
Fills thy mother garden.
How ego to thy head goes!

O thou rose of red hue!
Like disaster is thy eve.
Thy petals are scattered
All over the garden ground,
With thorns bleeding thee,
Like thy ego of red color,
That fills my being too, that
Meditation alone can cure.

SECTION V

Something about Myself

1. A Confession

Today do I a confession make
That I love you, and everything
OF yours—your parents, even your dog!
Also love I everything you love.
Love I everything that to you is
Attached, and this I do, though know
I that you love me not the least.
My heart waits not for a foreign
Stimulus, for instead of blood,
It is love that flows out for all.

2. Reprieve

How many times have I been born, and in how
Many forms of beings—as asp or ass, an eel,
Or an elephant or an eagle; how oft have
I tread, swum and flown as beasts, fish and birds
Or as stones, trees or rivulets been, till this
Human birth been granted with promise ever
To be true, and follow right pious pursuits.
But my youthful days this world of pleasures
Now has tempted away into every wayward way,
And pain of ailments now remind the end
Is round the corner, filling with fears that
Might I be thrown back into deserved void.
In this misty prison of passions, hear
I a holy hymn in a seer's serene voice,
Assuring hope that the Lord might grant another
Chance, and so do I pray for a reprieve.

3. The Moss

Wish I were a stone,
Tho' with softer heart,
That a creature's pain
Could feel, and could cure.

Wish I were a stone,
That a boy could kick,
Or hammer might break,
Or could, wirh water, flow.

Perhaps the boy's kick,
Or the hammer's hit,
Or moving with brook,
Remove my mind's moss
Gathered all my life.
Beside the moss, haven't
I so many vices more
That block needle's eye
A camel can pass through.

4. Thoughts Near Ana Sagar

Ajmer Visited After Fifty years

Fifty years are gone, and after fifty winters
Round the states, have I come again to our town's
Ana Sagar to watch its watery waves
That I as a boy in the rainy season
Always enjoyed, but, O Lord! this time it's all
Gone dry, there're no waves nor watery murmurs.
Look I up at the Hanuman Mandir, and
On barran hill nearby, that impresses
With its white airy Circuit House above,
Dazzling like a crown of silver. That goat
Tries a dry twig to be one with nature!
There's the white-marbled Bara Dari Jahagir
Built the full lake to enjoy with his queen,
And also to pray to appease Allah for crimes
Done. Once again go I down the green garden
That once Daulat Bagh was, now called Netaji
Park, and provides still a pleasing sight and shade gives.
On a summer afternoon, while like olden days
Of boyhood freedom, near the fountain I
Sit, and reflect on things that never earlier
Had visited this mind, for lonely now feels
My heart at the constant stabs of mortality:
At the disappearance of near and dear ones,
And the shock my darling Jeet's going has been.
So easily eyes get wet, but that's the way.
Know I not when ends this waiting period.
After autumn's robbing do come fresh green leaves,
As vacancy by death by new life is filled,
And life's transient sorrows by joys replaced!

5. Fruitful Would My Life Be

Fruitful would my life be
If, for one in pain,
A sure cure could I be.

Fruitful would my life be
If, to an orphan, food,
Lamp, books could I provide.

Fruitful would my life be
If, by my jokes, could I
Banish worries of all.

Fruitful would my life be
If, for a breaking couple,
Could I a strong glue be.

How I long, in every face,
To see the same Light,
That from Heaven descends!

SECTION VI

From History

1. Two Hundred and Thirty Nine Years to the Panth

Nanak, blessed with the Lord's Divine Light,
Spread His message far and wide over the globe,
Dispelling darkness of untruth, strife,
And hateful bloodsheds between man and man.
Preaching instead how best to live one's life
As a family man, without escaping
One's worldly duties, and social life, but
Earning by hard labour, and sharing bread
With any needy person, and meditating over
The One Eternal GOD, the CREATOR of all,
And to one's own religion remain true.
He, the first Nanak, in nine other bodies,
But as the same 'jyot' (Light) the message
Of the Lord did in musical hymns record
And spread among all humanity. Hence Nanak
Passed his 'jyot' on to tried worthy
And obedient Lehna, uplifting him
As his own Angad (own limb), and his successor.
Guru Angad a new script created for
His Master's hymns, and 'akharas' he started
For healthier youth, and spread Sikh faith, with Mata
Khiwi enlarging Nanak's 'Sacha Sauda'.
Became he the Preceptor to Amar-
Das, the symbol of Service, Shelter for
The Homeless, and Strenth for the weak.
He as third Nanak insisted that all first
Take food in Pangat before his Sangat;
Forbade he cruel 'Sati' practice, and raised he
The esteem of women, "from whom are born
Kings". Guru Amar Das established centres
Many in many parts to spread Nanak's message.
Orphan Ram Das he raised from poverty,
Made him his son-in-law, and next Guru,
Who from a pond created the Sarovar of 'Amrit',
Midst which lake later his third son, Arjun Dev,
With Waheguru's grace, the holy Harmandir made.

Guru Amar Das had known that his grandson
Arjun Dev had divine height, and love for
Gurbani and blessed him, who as Guru,
Did the largest hymns add to the Adi Geanth,
The 'Pothi' that then contained the 'bani' of
First five Gurus, with hymns Guru Nanak
Of some earlier saints had collected, along
With other votaries of the faith, and bhatts.
Amritsar he into thriving business centre
Made, where flocked around him Hindu-Muslim
Faithfuls, which irritated bigoted Jahangir.
To him the Guru's emphasis on Truth was
Just 'trading in falsehood'; hence was arrested
The saint, and impossible terms were imposed
On the Guru, who instead death preferred to
Conversion to Islam. Seated was he
On a burning iron sheet, with red hot sands
Showered from above on his body, thereafter
Steamed in boiling water. Thus was tortured
He for five long days, and then into the cold
Waters of Ravi thrown. Is it possible
To conceive a death crueler even for a devil?
But to Guru Arjun Dev, deep in Lord's thoughts,
This was only sweet, being the will of the Lord.
From God sought he only blessings of His Name.
The next Guru his son Har Gobind he made
Who, realizing 'twas time for change, wore swords
Of 'miri' and 'piri', and with a small band
Of brave inspired men wiped out large enemy
Forces in battles everytime. He also built
Akal Takht in front of Har Mandir's Darshan
Deori, from where to issue 'hukumnamas'.
After his deceitful imprisonment, he came out
Only as the 'bandi-chhor' of fifty-two princes.
He didn't permit even his sons Gurfitta and
Attal interfere with God's will, and they did
On their father's behest give up their lives.
Hence was chosen Gurditta's son, the humble,
Tender lover of nature—Har Rai as

The next Guru, who on his son Ram Rai's
'Be-Imani' with Gurbani disowned him, and
Passed Guruship on to the five year old
Har Kishan, the dispeller of suffering,
Whose bungalow in Delhi the Bangla
Sahib shrine became, who serving the sick
Himself died, declaring 'Baba Bakala'
As next Guru, whom Makhan Shah Labana
Eureka-ed as the long meditating Tegh Bahadur.
The new Nanak awakened people to
Fight against injustice for their rights, and built
Back their religious temples, by the Mughal emperor
Destroyed. For the Hindu 'jeneo' laid he
Down his life as "Hind di chaddar", saving
Various faiths of India turning into 'green'.
His nine year old Gobind Rai as his heir
He had made, whose martyred father's head only
Inspired to fire 'weak birds' with Amrit to
Fight unholy hawks. In his short life, produced
The 'Sant-Sipahi' poetry divine, and when
Challenged, recreated the Holy Granth, and
Gave 'Jaap' too, that narrates myriads ways God
Runs His worlds. Amrit he blessed his 'Piaras',
And from them sought the same, thus from Guru
Their 'chela' became, world's only such instance
Of the kindler becoming the kindled!
His young sons Ajit and Jhujhar at Chamkaur
Fighting forces, and Fateh and Zoravar at
Sirhind walled alive, with their grieved grand-mother
Falling from the 'cold burj'. The 'Vansdani'
Lost them all for his country's freedom! But
With 'Zafar-nama' shamed the zealot Emperor
Thus reducing to shambles his empire!
Before merging with the Divine Lord, he
At Nander ended further living line
Of Gurus, and declared thst the Khalsa Panth
Has been created on the Lord's Command, and
Henceforth shall the Granth, God's Word lead the Panth!"
Good conduct and meditation on Lord's Name

Alone shall rid man of further comings and
Goings. Thus was the new Panth by Nanaks
Raised, with Granth's message not only for Sikhs,
And not merely for the people of India,
But for the guidance of all humanity.

2. Fact or Fiction?

The rural singer this tale used to tell
Of King Bal, grand-son of Bhagat Prehlad.
He conquered had Indrapuri,
The kingdom of gods, and their king Indra.
'Welcome!' 'Bravo!' Applauded the very sky,
As King Bal caught the cheat tight by his feet.
Brahma, as disguised pigmy, had come, where
The king was performing a grand 'yagna'
On conquering the domain of King Indra.
As the benevolent Bal sought the lad's wish
As gift to the Brahmin at yagna's close,
After many entreaties, begged the boy just
For two and a half strides of land outside
The gate of the palace, there to sit and
Sing eulogies of the valiant old king.
The victorious Bal, the readers do know,
Was the grandson of Prahlad, to save whom
God had sprung out, as Narsinh, half lion and
Half man, from a gigantic pillar
And had Harnakash, Prahlad's father torn
With bare nails for trying to injure His
Prahlad. The saint and then his son had reigned
As saint-kings for centuries, and served well
Their public and the Lord. Now had King Bal
Proved himself as their worthy successor.
Beguiled by demand of a petty piece of land
By the pigmy, Bal conceded had his gift.
But the Brahmin in disguise was Brahma,
Who his true form in no time had assumed
And covered in only two gigantic strides
Bal's entire vast kingdom, and then asked for
Land worth half remaining stride. Baffled
Though, Bal did lay himself down on the ground
Offering his own body as half remainin' stride.
The cunning Brahma, thereupon, with his foot
Pushed Bal down into Patal, the under-world.

Undaunted remained Bal, lost not his cool,
And tightly clung to Brahma's pushing foot,
Wise Bal reminded the god of his vow
Of singing eulogies at palace gate.
In his plight, descended from the heavens,
Vishnu and Mahesh to rescue Brahma.
The three gods pleaded with Bal, and
Pulling him out, promised to sit outside
Palace gate, four months each, every year and sing
Praises of Bal; which promise they still keep.
"Truly", says rural singer, "God's saints are
Mightier than all gods, for saints are His equal.

3. The Longest Saree

In an hour of outrageous disgrace, was
She, dragged by her tresses, into the court
Of the blind King, the sire of a hundred,
Who sat with a mate, who blind-folded had
Her eyes to equal the Lord's injustice to her husband.
Dropadi's husbands the disgrace done to her
Watched as five mute helpless witnesses, For Yadhuster had gambled
their Daropadi,
His four brothers and himself away as slaves
To Daryodhan. so sat the five humbled
As their Daropadi was dragged into the presence
Of the King by the wicked Dushashan.
But quietly the greats of the times—Bhisham
Pitama, the clan's most revered Elder.
Also watched the Rishi Guru, who trained
Had hundred Kauravas, and five Pandavas.
Silent sat too other gems of the court.
Yudhister, Truth Personified, Bhim, the
Tower of muscular power, Arjan, bowman
Excellent, who shot had a revolving
Fish's eye with his arrow to win Daropadi,
The beautiful, in the 'swamver', and on
His mother's innocent remark, had shared
Her with the other four! Thus was she made 'Panchali'!
Lost had they moral fibre and glory,
And knew not anyway to save her honour.
After man unshielded remains by man, turns
He to the Almighty, and prays to be saved.
When, in her distress, she ultimately called
Upon her Krishna, came He in no time
To her rescue, and flowed out a saree that
Went on and on and on and had no end!
Dropadi was by the unseen Krishna saved!

4. The Temple that Turned Around

To his Beethal's temple at Pindalpur
Came 'low-caste' Namdev, the calico-printer
On whom was by God sainthood bestowed.
The Brahmin priests beat the poor saint away, and
Let saint Namdev not enter the temple.
As a child had he realized that the Lord
In every heart breathes, and does everywhere exist.
He had loved Him as loved had the child Dhru,
And Prahlad. In many a place and various
Forms had Namdev seen visions of the Lord.
He in Dwarka of Lord Krishna had met
Him as a Mughal in Pathan's 'pagri'.
An elephant, goaded to trample Namdev
To death, on the Lodhi King's command, saw him
As the Lord's own man and lifted him up in
Salutation, despite mohavat's many attempts
By him made on King's commands, all because
Namdev would perform no miracle, nor would
He be forced to utter 'Allah', though often
Namdev called his Beethal by Muslim name.
When he tried the temple at Pinderpur
That morning to enter, the priests did all block
Way to the shrine, and even did beat him up;
They would not an 'untouchable' let enter
The temple, so did Nama go to the backyard,
And sat down in deep worship of Beethal.
It thus happened then that the Lord turned around
The temple, so that the deity faced Namdev!
Thus were humbled the arrogant 'upper-caste'
Brahmans and the devotee was honoured.
Before Him are all men equal, and their
Distinctions mean nothing in the Lord's court.

SECTION VII

Sonnets

1. Love in the Sky

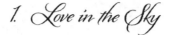

All at once above the waters of the lake
Enchanted saw I the snow-white sea-gull,
Frolicking around in the strong blowing breeze,
Circling and teasing the watchers in the boat.
Though wings were tired, but ecstatic was the spirit.
On the mast it rests, where flutters the flag
Of the land; on my camera I too then
Capture the images of the perching bird.
But all hear, of a sudden, its male's cry
And refreshed, in a shrill note of frenzy,
Soars it up and chirping meets its love-mate,
And, in a love ecstatic that fills up
Human hearts too, they vanish into the sky.
So does this heart pine to fly and search her.

2. On the Winged Dreams

Come, do come, lighted day's reliever;
In its cave, sun's horses to rest are gone.
Stars on the azure above stealthily appear
To balm our body, tho' not the soul's fever.
My tired body a pillow and your darkness
Welcomes; won`t you let your sweet daughter now
In my bed slip, and kissing my wet eyes,
Lead me to a land of romantic dreams.
On her light wings every day a far-off land
I reach to meet my departed darling-
A trip so desperately have I cherished.
Some moments thus from her death's silence stolen.
Day drags; how pine I to greet the black beauty,
Wrapped up in her burqa of black silk!

3. Alarm Before Dawn

As stars plan their retreat before dawn`s glow,
From their sleeping nests come out the small birds
On to the window-sill of my bed-room
And do their sweet musical chorus begin.
Their sound's an old man's alarm in waking sleep;
Hearken I their choral, that I know conveys
To the Lord their gratitude for sheltering
The nestlings as fly they far away for food.
O my winged friends! Take not yet your flight;
But in your warbling, add my prayers too-
My pleadings that He, on my exit from earth,
No further births may in future ordain.
O Lord Merciful! Bestow on me Thy boon
And of transmigration this evil soul free.

4. Like a Dream is Life

This hot night this summer a wondrous dream
Of a future unknown floated before my eyes
That among cheering dears a huge chocolate cake
On his birthday was my dear friend cutting.
An octogenarian had he that night become!
What a moment of delight 'twas for all!
The hotel did like ever festive look wear,
With guests their plates noisily with tasty eats
Piling. Yet, as they hungrily were about
To start to eat, a shriek of a dying man
Broke the din of the crowded hall and all
Rushed to where the birthday boy ceased to breathe.
Amid female gossip, and cheers of all friends,
Was I stuffing birthday boy a big piece.

5. A Star in the Sky

Staggering, step by small step, the blithe soul
Reclining on her nurse's shoulder, moved she
Out of her room to her mate with a smile,
Ignorant of her brief earthly sojourn's end.
Feeble was her voice, but on her face a glow
Showed not the strife of a suffering life;
Attempted to conceal pain, but on her brow
Shone satisfying designs of devotion.
"I've come", whispered she, and collapsed into
Awaiting arms; it was the farewell embrace
Of this sojourn. Earth its dust had claimed
And skyward had the star of my heart moved.
No secret is it that man is mortal.
But such sudden departures God's tease are.

6. Portrait of My Lady

Why was it that painter in me that night,
When my beautiful bride that moment clung
To me in a flush of deepest desire?
Why thought I not drawing her in color?
Covering my eyes with her long tresses,
Whisper'd she what never before had she done.
A sensation through my body had passed
And I to my heart had compressed my dame.
Exhibitions of my creations, plenty
Connoisseurs of art have ever been drawing,
Enriching my coffers and the attentions
Of female admirers too have my ego ballooned.
But the thought of that warming coy embrace
My darling gave then ever enlivens my dreams.

7. Shall I Tell You?

Shall I tell you why am I so enamoured
When arise 'fore my eyes the magnificent
Dazzling vision of Himalaya's snow-capped peaks
Piercing the high heavens in full brilliance?

Shall I tell you how my heart with joy jumps
When races a rivulet down a steep high mount
Into a gorge, and a rainbow on vapours
Of the gorgeous water-fall is so created?

How sight of Lucy do I love, as she
Coyly her first kiss tastes her lover plants
In hot flush of love, and takes willing lass
In a clumsy embrace, lost to the world!

Shall I tell you how all such sights my heart
With pleasure fill? No, I don't have the words!

8. I Slept Not That Night

I could not for a moment sleep that night;
A bird`s melancholy dirge did bleed my heart
As the nightingale, by its mate deserted,
Damyanti-like Nul's disappearance bewailed.
My own heart, which of its own wounds, does bleed
Lets but lightly sleep, joins ever the suffering
Of any grieving soul, did the whole night weep
Till just after dawn, the bird`s lover returned.
Quiet now its song was, and the twain had gone
Far, far away; and the house had a new day
Begun; soon were all on different ways gone.
At the window sit I and watch the world.
"When a joy does in your heart bloom", say saints,
"Thank the Lord; thank Him also when a thorn pricks."

9. By Your Leave

Have I your leave to call thee my darling
And may towards you a flying kiss throw?
Why don't you, readily like a blissful cloud,
A loving drizzle any moment dost spray?
Why do your eyes, that with drugged fluid are filled,
Never twinkle like a romantic heroine's?
Long are your locks long I to caress long;
Now in embrace, no more flying kisses!
We are, like birds of some moments, that soon
The Reaper at His fixed hour shall snatch away.
No time have we in any wrangles to waste;
No meaningless talks. no routines but love.
As long as we still breathe, or eyes do see,
Let's waste no time, but spare it all for love.

10. Live Life as it Comes

Oft mourned have bards of age, disease and death,
Of blood-baths of wars, defeats and disgrace,
False hope, female frailty, unfriendly foes
And darts of sorrow, pain, death and rebirth.
Musical melody makes for deepest
poetry—
A mix of pain and pleasure, hate and love,
Depths and heights, births and deaths, wars and peace-pacts.
With birth comes man's fate as Lord has preplanned
As deemed just for past deeds and misdeeds;
Triumph o'er temptations and remembering
Him might cleanse past ills, if the Lord is pleased.

So shall I seek in prayers blessings that
I might grateful be for His every design.

11. In Memory of My Mentor

Mr. Bhupendra Hooja, I.A.S. (Retd)

The gurgling surging waters and the ark
That smoothly flow, and above them the pilot
Whose urging note carries a spark in it
That hear all on far off coast and islet.

The ark of talented scholars does brim
Steered by the pilot as if gondola;
His clarion call sounds as a hymn
To honour careers of the tricolor.

Dozing was I my days on dryland;
Forgetful was I of the pen I held;;
He shook me with a pat of his hand,
My sleeping pen some wordly craft to weld.

Silent lays the pilot, but I do hear
The pilot's blessing, "Thy pen will ever create".

12. On a Lady—Love's Demise

She was like a joyful bird, but her cheer,
That ever did spread around, now doth spread no more.
Forever does she now rest on a dusty bed
In an unlit small vault in the cemetery.
Deserted lies now her old humming place;
Weeds wildly grow, with dust blocking the door.
Her phone`s dumb, and no friends in evenings come. Cockroaches there
do full monopoly enjoy.
Cold, dark, and lonely is this her new room;
But here too has she friends surrounding her—
Those maggots that feed on her beauteous remains,
Reducing them to dust, that mortals are.
A loving heart daily visits her grave
To whisper things, to place a wreath and pray.

13. Wordsworth, Thou Shouldst Be Living at this Hour

Wordsworth, thou shouldst be living at this hour;
Not England, but Ind has need of thee.
Prosaic is our time; our eyes are not free
To watch a sheep, a bird, or a flower!

In fields see we no solitary reaper-
Tractor has her replaced; a butterfly
No charm hath, nor to save Lucy we try;
Shallow are we, like a worthless creeper.

Leaps not our heart; bye-pass stops us to;
Rising late, morning walks how can we take?
Parties late for drinks and cards we have
And no healthy, but junk food do we love.

This's no time that you could rest; wake, O awake;
Get out of your grave, and initiative take!

14. Wonder Where They Live

For years had I wondered where they lived,
Had feed 'n' fodder, were milked and did breed,
For never did they ever parade the roads
Of Brampton, or did on any highway shit.
My eyes hunger'd have sight of Mother Cow,
Or of her husband, easily found roaming
Chaura Rasta, or M.I. Road or on
A congested traffic circle squatting.
Kids here think milk, butter and yogurt,
Like packets of ice-cream of all types and
Flavours, come for them machine—manufactured,
As do come here various products from China.
Sitting at my window, day-dream I now
The rising vision of holy Mother Cow!

15. On Watching "Baghban" Again

Why watched I that movie 'gain tonight
Of the old loving parents, by their sons
Separated? That was done only once for six months,
And they were together again. I might
Too have borne the pangs of a lonely life
With hope of meeting her again somewhere,
But that's not to be. She's gone now where
Shall I be when He finds me tired of strife.

Stars are bright, and moonlight washes my room;
The maple trees are quiet, no chirping birds sing.
In some slumbering house, they wake and cling
Passionately together. And in the gloom
All hope rests on Him to meet my Jeetiya-
It is a fatigued, pining man's only goal.

16. They were not Rats

No rats, but humans they killed those three days.
Centuries will pass, but none can forget
The brutal murders, loot, rapes, and arson,
When quietly slept a son's law and order.

None came to rescue Sikhs dragged from their homes,
Loaded with burning tyres, or stabbed to death.
Killed were thousands, widowed, orphaned and homeless
Rendered, and till now awaiting justice!

'Twas said a giant BANYAN tree had fallen,
With natural consequences: some rats were crushed;
Their Har Mandir desecrated and Har Gobind's
Akal Takht demolished, at pigmy command.

How easy to forget the 'Sis Ganj' of Delhi,
Whose blood 'jenew' saved, and land from turning' green!

17. They were Barbaric Savages who Looted

They were barbaric savages who looted,
Destroyed, demolished and defiled
The Holy of Holies, but retreating faced the
Brave, who an unforgettable lesson taught.

How can one forget the sixth June, when a
Draconian, 'democratic' hand had razed,
Erased, and attempted to destroy Sikh psyche?
Thousands were burnt alive at the Banyan's fall.

Blinded, brutalised, leaving widows and
Orphans, burnt houses and shops: victims
Still await a verdict true against the vandals-
Leaders and marauders, who commited crimes.

By their blood, doth their Sanctum returned is
To its glory, and the phoenix is reborn.

SECTION VIII

Limericks

1. There always were from Jhumri Talaya
   Some 'farmaish' for a song of Suraiya,
   And it was ever played,
   Request that was made
   For her songs from Jhumri Talaya.

2. Close friends interned him here-under,
   But they later realized their blunder,
   For lovable noble James Rice,
   Who was exceedingly nice,
   And the poor fellow had even not dyed!

3. Once an old clergyman, Mr. High
   Praised God's marvel, the house fly,
   Which grateful insect rose
   And sneaked into the nose
   Of the highly reputed Mr. High.

4. The beautiful young lady of Koem
   To her friend dictated a poem
   About the confessions
   Of an owl's passions,
   And had him sign under the poem.

5. That young wise lady from News Center,
   Got her car done by a denter;
   Needing it painted
   After 'twas dented
   Straight went she to the carpenter.

6. That strange old man from Samrella,
   Known as the fool with umbrella,
   Which lesked in the rains,
   And in summers a bane
   'Twas, like that fool from Sambrella.

7. To the thief Ram gave such a chase,
   His friends clapped his run in praise,
   And as Ram reached close,
   Thief stopp'd, but he chose
   To run on, hearing only the praise.

8. That tipsy fat man of Dinapur
   Slipp'd and fell in heavy downpour
   In a pretty deep drain;
   Kiran brought a crane
   To rescue that fool of Dinapur.

9. Fell that old man of Timbuktu
   For a young lass, straight as bamboo;
   Ere guessing how she felt,
   Proposed, but him she dealt
   A blow, whereupon cried he, "U2!"

10. A frail voice came from that old grave;
    Feared I there was a skinny hand-wave;
    Or was it a hand-shake
    Or sought that piece of cake
    That I was eating near her grave.

11. That old lady was at the window
    Waiting for her husband to go.
    They bitterly had fought;
    Of suicide she had thought,
    Jumped down, but became a widow.

12. When that old tycoon proposed
    To the lass who on beach reposed;
    "All right," she at once said,
    "Your proposal's not bad,
    If first you get your hag divorced".

13. "What momento's here?", asked doctor,
    Pointing to the locket of Mrs Kaur.
    "O hubby's hair, doc",
    "Isn't he alive?" Asks doc.
    "Alive 'n' kicking, but gone bald, doctor!"

14. That cricket fan with a turban,
    Enjoying one-dayer in Durban;
    To applaud the six
    By his friend Dremix,
    Couldn't raise hat, that man in turban.

15. In Delhi lived that young girl Sue,
    Dull in school, but fashionable grew;
    When they said," You're nice",
    She would quote her price!
    At her place, though, they made a
    Q
      U
        e
          u
            e.

SECTION IX

Haikus

1. When the cop by Tom
    Was told he was killing time,
    The cop arrested him.

2. The dog-bit man roamed
    Freely in the curfew area,
    Thinking 'twas dog-free.

3. He always sets the stage
    On fire; hence they always keep many
    Fire-extinguishers ready.

4. There's no difference
    Between your arguments and a
    Sieve; neither holds water!

5. Relish bacteria
    If you like, but first mix it
    With milk, then rest it

6. Members applaud when
    The guy breaks ice in the club,
    Without use 'ova' club.

7. The guy keeps no cent,
    For his trousers have pockets
    None for a wallet.

8. People can't over-hear
    Through a wall, if 'tis made of
    Pure solid concrete.

9. I thought she was wise;
    Huge was her head, but scanning
    Showed it was empty.

10. Fear not too many cooks
    In kitchen; just get cooked no
    Broth, but rice and curry.

11. God's reported to have
    Created universe in six days,
    Then gave us Sunday.

12. Absence long from home
    Makes hearts fonder, if neighbors
    Are true Christians too.

13. I felt that this fairy
    Was so fair it was fair enough
    That I fall for her.

14. When to him proposed
    The black beauty, "O.K.", thought he,
    "Only light will cost more."

15. When she proposed, prompt
    Was his reply: "I will not make
    The same mistake once".

16. If all your books are
    Like a pretty lady's looks, will they
    Really teach you much?

17. "Can you tell me why
    Black sheep eat less than the white?"
    "Idiot, they're so few."

18. God! Give lots of flesh
    On my darling, so that I
    Don't ever feel her dearth.

19. When this farmer starved
    To death, many leaders shed tears
    Of so many crocodiles.

20. When asked his address,
    Said the old man of Oslo,
    'Tis "S3L 1HO".

21. As bright shines the sun,
    Reflects the moon that its light
    Is mere reflection!

22. Don`t the ladies fear
    They aren't by nature pretty, or
    Would parlors charge sky?

23. Never do call a dog
    'Son of a bitch', for that will
    Sure offend the dogma.

24. When a public man
    To a pub goes, he feels like
    Licking something there.

25. When it rains like cats
    And dogs, wonder who pushes
    Them down from the clouds.

26. Asked what best he drew,
    Promptly said the paid painter,
    "Of course, my salary!"

27. These days a damsel
    Can manage marketing too;
    She can sell a dam!

28. Aunt Wendy isn't candid;
    All find her very very pretty;
    She is just not plain.

29. Maghna is very proud;
    She is full of airs, thinking
    She's a music book.

30. Aren't M.Ps getting
    Sports-minded? they don't discuss,
    But throw a discus.

31. Anne's d.o.b is ever
    Static; she's still as young as
    She was at sexteen!

32. Are not policemen like
    Rainbows? Yes, they also arrive
    When the storm is over.

33. Isn't Tom Bigger's son
    Bigger than his Dad? Yes, he
    Is a little Bigger.

34. The reason of Anne's
    Decreasing brains: she's ever parting
    With 'pieces of her mind'.

35. The hall was full, yet
    There wasn't a single person
    Present, only couples!

36. "Can you tell me what
    Expands when you contract it?"
    "Loan when contracted."

37. What have the Arabs there
    To live on in the desert?
    Sand-which is aplenty!

38. Don't you think that love
    is a deep pit? No doubt, yet
    Lovers keep falling.

39. Two sons had Adam and
    Eve, but Cain hated his brother
    As long he was Abel.

40. That fool is sitting
    And cutting same branch, hoping
    To turn a new leaf.

41. Om never lends anyone
    His ears; he knows that on it,
    He'll earn no interest.

42. When he asked them to
    Lend him their ears, they protested,
    "We want to hear you."

43. "Aren't flamingoes and
    Doctors alike?" "Yes, are their bills
    Not extremely big?"

44. Matrimony in U.S.A
    Turns Into alimony, the prize for
    The lady out of house.

45. The paws of a cat
    Have claws, as comma has its
    Pause after a clause.

46. Tom boasts that he never
    Bets like gambler Dick, and so,
    Isn't Tom some better?

47. Her dog is amazing
    For its six legs—has fore-legs
    In front 'n' two behind!

48. John is a thinker,
    And claims his ill-fed dog
    Too is a thin-cur.

49. Section one four four,
    Of Indian Penal Code, I think,
    Indeed is two gross.

50. A skyscraper can
    Make you a fiction writer;
    You get many a story.

51. A heart-broken poet
    Tries, sip by sip, to glue back
    Heart`s broken pieces.

52. A camel's back is
    Like a physical balance; hnows
    Weight of the last straw!

53. Isn't it foolish to
    Call a dark night a Sunday,
    Even if it really is!

54. Pray all peaceful men:
    "Let missiles of the anarchists
    Boomerang on them."

55. Casanova's reason for
    Giving up his steamy affairs
    Was loss of the steam.

56. 'Tis wonderful that
    Rickshaw-puller got
    elected!
    He did pull large crowds.

57. Cocks and crows are birds
    Completely different, yet cocks
    Do every morning crow.

58. When told a grandson
    To him was born, cried he, "How!
    I'm now a widower."

59. Mike alleges that Wiite
    Has bugged his house phone, so
    Calls him a bugger!

60.Last month this Portugeese
 Couple was blessed with their
 Third Portugoose son.

<hr>

I Am a Sikh

I am a Sikh, one out of over 25 million followers of Sikhism, the youngest of the major religions of the world, founded by Guru Nanak Dev in the later half of the fifteenth century, preaching a life of harmony, brotherhood, and tolerance. We believe in the ten Sikh Gurus from Guru Nanak Dev to Guru Gobind Singh, and are guided by Sri Guru Granth Sahib, the eternal Guru. We believe in one God, the Supreme Prime Being of all humanity. We call Him "Waheguru", go to a gurudwara, open to people of all castes, creeds, colors and ranks, and aspire to visit Sri Har Mandir Sahib of Amritsar. We are a warm, affectionate, hard-working, progressive, peace-loving and particularly enterprising people, spread all over the grobe. And we are against terrorism and fight for the weak. We pray for "sarbat da bhala" (the good of all humamity).

So am I proud to be a Sikh.